A Taylor & Me

JOURNAL

First published in Great Britain in 2025 by
Michael O'Mara Books Limited
9 Lion Yard
Tremadoc Road
London SW4 7NQ

A CIP catalogue record for this book is available from the British Library.

This product is made of material from well-managed, FSC®-certified forests
and other controlled sources. The manufacturing processes conform to the
environmental regulations of the country of origin.

ISBN: 978-1-78929-753-9 in paperback print format

2 3 4 5 6 7 8 9 10

Cover design by Natasha Le Coultre
Cover illustration by Alicia Nicole
Designed and typeset by Claire Cater and Natasha Le Coultre
Illustrated by Alicia Nicole

Printed and bound in China

www.mombooks.com

MIX
Paper | Supporting
responsible forestry
FSC® C010256

A Taylor & Me

JOURNAL

ERA BY ERA

UNOFFICIAL

ABI SMITH

Illustrated by **ALICIA NICOLE**

Michael O'Mara Books Limited

Introduction

Era by era, Taylor has taken us on a journey of her own self-discovery and learnings, from her authentic beginnings through a courageous journey of fighting for what she believes in. Along the way, she has pushed boundaries and celebrated the chaos of the conflicting emotions that make us human, brushing off negative aspects of her past.

She has shown she isn't afraid to celebrate the things she loves and explore her theatrical side, while her later albums have seen her reflect on the more heightened emotional periods of her journey.

In various iterations she has reinforced the message that it is always important to focus on trust and putting your own contentment first before you open up to others.

This journal is a way of linking Taylor's experiences and songs into areas of your own life – a collection of ideas and prompts to help you rise above times of frustration or heartbreak and focus on your tribe. It's a collection of helpful ways to remind you of the queen you are and ultimately to guide you to encompass a little bit of the Taylorverse into your everyday life.

You Are Exactly Where You Are Meant to Be

Taylor has never shied away from being herself, even if that means she has been considered too young and naive or too soppy and silly. In the song '22' she makes no excuses for celebrating her youth and living in the moment, but how many of us actually do that? Sometimes we're so busy looking to the past or the future or comparing ourselves to our friends, we forget to live in the moment. So, stop comparing and start living and enjoying what you are doing right now. Don't make yourself small for anyone — be funny, be kind, be the awkward, intelligent, beautiful little weirdo you are and don't hold back.

Make a list of things you are grateful for right at this moment in time — small crumbs of joy or big bites of happiness, it doesn't matter, just get listing.

Taylor tip: Plan a girls' night of cheesy board games and classic movies, or go for some real vintage fun and grab a bunch of duvets, some bottles of fizz and nail polish, and invite your girlfriends round for a sleepover!

Who are the people in your life that inspire you to do things? Who do you think you inspire? With those people in mind, make a to-do list of things you want to achieve in the next six months and how that will help you in the future.

Rise Above

Don't let others define you and have the confidence to own who you are — this is the strongest message Taylor gave us in her early career. Friendship is a number-one priority for the singer, who knows you can rise above setbacks and that you can't let other people's opinions of you influence your life or your happiness. There might be times when you face unfair scrutiny or when people will criticize choices you make or decisions you stand by, but the only people you really need to care about are yourself and the people you love. Later, 'It's Nice to Have a Friend' celebrates how beautiful authentic friendships can be, so find your squad, the ones who matter — and forget the rest!

We can't control how other people view us, so we just have to let them think or act how they want to — it has no bearing on us or our decisions. Write about how you can let someone be wrong about you. What evidence do you have from your life that shows you what they're saying isn't true? How can you listen to your own voice rather than theirs?

_____

_____

_____

_____

_____

_____

_____

_____

_____

_____

_____

_____

_____

_____

_____

_____

_____

_____

_____

_____

_____

_____

Taylor tip: Gather round your closest friends and go out dancing. Dance out any negativity or low vibes that have tried to bring you down and remind yourself how fabulous you are. Don't feel like going out? No need — turn up the speakers at home and get dancing around the kitchen without a care in the world about what you look like or who's watching.

Share the Stage

While everything Taylor does has her unique stamp
on it, she loves to collaborate and work with women
who inspire her or celebrate her music and want to
showcase it as best they can. She is a feminist icon
and is happy to share the stage with other global
superstars, Hollywood actresses and world-famous
musicians because she knows that what they can
create together is more powerful. Telling people they
inspire you or reaching out to your role models is a
positive thing, a way of saying to the universe, 'This
place is big enough for everyone to shine!' She knows
that womanhood isn't a competition and that we are
strongest when we cheer each other on, raise each
other up and celebrate and respect each other.

We meet phenomenal women every single day in every area of our lives — family, friends, colleagues, neighbours, old school teachers etc. — and it would be a shame if we didn't tell them at every opportunity we can. Use this space to draft a letter to a woman in your life who has inspired or positively influenced you, or give them a videocall and tell them to their face.

Pass on a random act of kindness next time you see a stranger — for example, why not buy a hot drink for the person behind you in the queue or drop round a bunch of flowers to an elderly neighbour? Remind people that it takes nothing to be kind and polite. Make a list of random acts of kindness you'd like to do.

Taylor tip: Hold your own 'Women's Day' and invite round all the women you know. Just because!

Speak Up

Just as Taylor showcased in her 2010–12 golden era, by experimenting with style and sound and blending genres of music beyond her precious country-pop style, you too can be a glorious mixture of emotions and complexities. You'll find certain friends will embrace your wild and adventurous side, while you'll love to spend time with other pals when you're in need of sound advice and companionship. Make sure you find your authentic friends who embrace all the wonderful complexities you contain: wild but shy, happy but free — and don't be defined by one label.

Ask your friends what they like about you and why. Write them down and celebrate these traits other people see in you, and remember them when others dismiss them. Do the same for your friends.

_____

_____

_____

_____

_____

_____

_____

_____

_____

_____

Taylor tip: Spend time acknowledging people who have made a difference in your life. Maybe send them a voicenote or tag them in a post with a photo of you both to share your thanks. Put that positivity out into the world!

Think of some things you want to do but haven't because you fear it would raise a few eyebrows. For example, are you keen to join a sewing club or a women's rugby team but never quite been sure what others might think? Or are you desperate to dye your hair but are worried about disapproving looks? In three words, go for it! Make a list of your dream activities below.

Set Boundaries

Sometimes our friends do things we don't agree with or that we feel we have to put up with because we don't want to lose their friendship. 'Mean' is a song that calls out all the bullies and haters, while Taylor's later songs reinforce the message that in life there will be people you won't be able to trust. That's why personal boundaries and trying not to people please all the time is OK! Sometimes, with certain people, there is nothing left to say and no energy left to give — so think about whether their values align with yours, and if not, consider stepping back. Like Taylor says in 'Bad Blood', betrayal can't always be fixed or easily forgotten ... what friendships have cut you so deeply that it's time to wave goodbye for good?

What do you do to help friends when they need you? Are you a practical friend or do you offer advice and solace? Write down the ways you're a good friend to the people around you. Are there any ways you could be a better friend?

Taylor tip: Celebrate your tribe just because you can: make the friendship bracelets, send the messages, book the girly holiday ... you won't regret it.

Taylor values friendship, trust and respect — what values do you look for in friends? Make a list of your core values and why they are important to you.

This Is Why We Can't Have Nice Things

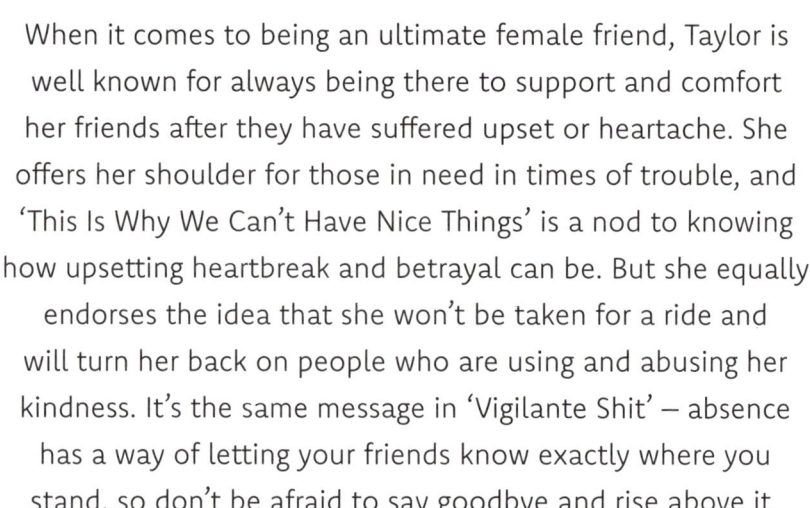

When it comes to being an ultimate female friend, Taylor is well known for always being there to support and comfort her friends after they have suffered upset or heartache. She offers her shoulder for those in need in times of trouble, and 'This Is Why We Can't Have Nice Things' is a nod to knowing how upsetting heartbreak and betrayal can be. But she equally endorses the idea that she won't be taken for a ride and will turn her back on people who are using and abusing her kindness. It's the same message in 'Vigilante Shit' – absence has a way of letting your friends know exactly where you stand, so don't be afraid to say goodbye and rise above it.

Explore strategies you can put in place to protect yourself against feeling other people's critiques too deeply. Their opinion is not yours to carry. List ways you can prioritize your own joy and leave the criticism behind.

_____

_____

_____

_____

_____

_____

_____

_____

_____

Taylor tip: Take time off social media for a while and see which friends you want to meet up with IRL rather than via social media. Perhaps it's time to let go of certain people in your life?

Have you been hanging on to a certain friendship because you think you should? Do you owe this person your time and effort? Do they make an effort when it comes to seeing you? If it's all a bit one-sided, it might be time to re-evaluate. Make a note of your thoughts.

I Did Something Bad

Taylor's late twenties brought a clear change in musical style as she leaned into electropop influences and R&B vibes. She began writing these angrier songs in response to the media scrutiny she received following the enormous success of her earlier albums. Just like in her song 'I Did Something Bad', there might be times when you doubt yourself, but you have to trust in the process. Breaking up a relationship is always going to be hard and you might feel guilty, but you don't know what the future holds. Feeling bad over ending relationships that weren't meant to be doesn't make you a bad person who doesn't know their own mind; it makes you human.

Jot down times when you feel you have done something 'bad' or something you feel guilty about. Take some time to journal about each thing and when you are ready, get a red pen and cross them out to signify that you have drawn a line under them and that they no longer have power to make you feel bad.

_____

_____

_____

_____

_____

_____

_____

_____

_____

Taylor tip: When times are especially tough, practise some breathing exercises to regulate your mood — sometimes these are best done alone or outside.

Use this page as your go-to for ideas when you need to reset yourself, so you always have an immediate source of inspiration. For example, keep a list of things that help you if you are triggered by a memory of an ex. Or keep handy a playlist of Taylor songs that will lift your mood instantly ...

Things Will Begin Again

Even after the most difficult of life experiences, such as heartbreak, Taylor teaches us that life can begin again. No feeling or emotion is permanent — sometimes it's about accepting that a certain chapter has finished, but don't forget that you have a whole book still to read. Just like Taylor sang about the hope of falling in love, sometimes it is in the quietest moments after a break-up that you can learn how to dust yourself off and not be afraid to put yourself out there again.

Poetry is a really good way to explore and jot down jumbled thoughts because you'll find they will soon form their own structure. Try forming verses or writing a haiku of your thoughts. This can help condense what you might consider to be a complex thought, as writing it down can help you simplify it.

Why not focus on things that have made you smile recently or made you laugh? Find at least one positive in each day and record what they are, no matter how small or trivial.

Like a Comfy Cardigan

Putting on your favourite cardi or snuggly hoodie can sometimes be all you need to be transported to a safe, happy place. People and memories can make you feel like this, too. Taylor's song 'Cardigan' might be about looking back on long-lost love, but there can be great comfort in exploring memories, people or times in your life that have shaped who you are today. Sometimes, of course, these reflections might require an extra layer of cardi comfort, but they are worth delving into …

What activities give you reassuring, cosy hug vibes and transport you back to times of peace? List them here.

_____

_____

_____

_____

_____

_____

_____

What can you do right now to give yourself a bit of comfort? How do you bring comfort to other people when they need it?

_____

_____

_____

_____

What times can you look back on in a different light now — maybe they were painful when they happened, but now you see them as shaping who you are?

Go for the Good

Lyrically, 'The Way I Loved You' is Taylor singing about being in a relationship with someone who is seemingly perfect for her, but she feels nothing for them. She wants the guy who is messy and frustrating, the bad boy – because the 'good' guy is just a little boring. Finding the right balance between someone who lights up your world but creates a fire in your belly can be hard, but it's not impossible. No one is all good or all bad, it's just that you might have to dig a little deeper into each trait – sometimes people don't want to showcase a part of themselves that is 'really them' for fear of exposing themselves to heartache.

Do you always go for someone who isn't necessarily a right fit for you because you like the excitement or 'bad vibes'? Why do you think that is? Perhaps you are waiting for your own 'Love Story' or fairytale romance? The key is to be honest with yourself about what you want in a partner and why. Think about your past romantic partners — what traits have they had in common and what do they draw out in you?

_____

_____

_____

_____

_____

_____

_____

_____

_____

_____

_____

Do you worry you will get bored if you always have someone who is dependable? Do you need to be with someone who you can argue with because expressing yourself in passionate exchanges and fiery outbursts excites you? List all the qualities that you look for in a partner now — are there more nice or naughty traits?

Champagne Problems

Taylor acknowledges that two people can have two very different plans for the same night: one to break up and one to propose. Sometimes we do grow apart from each other in a relationship, but the key to not being in complete shock at how things end up is communication. It's easy to avoid tackling difficult subjects with your partner — but don't wait until the champagne cork has popped and there's no going back!

'All Too Well' likewise narrates the course of an ultimately failed relationship. Taylor sings of the disconnect between her boyfriend's imagined version of herself compared to the reality and asks for honesty between the two of them. This is one of her most popular songs because it confronts the difficult truth of communication in relationships — but hard things can be worked through. You have the power!

Communication can be lost between the people we love the most — or it can be hard to say things we have been thinking for a while as time makes the issue bigger in our own minds than it actually is. Write down what you would like to say to your partner (or another important person in your life) but never have. Maybe when you write things down you'll realize that actually, in the cold light of day, they're not worth your energy.

Speak to your partner and ask them a question you want to know the answer to — something random but personal. You never know where that conversation will lead. If you are single, find a way of speaking to someone you fancy from afar ... What would you say to them? How would you strike up a conversation? Jot down a few ideas of things you might like to ask.

No One Gets Everything Right

As tempting as it is to think that Taylor is the sort of person who knows exactly what she is doing every single moment of every single day, no one gets it right all the time. Her longevity is something that can't be explained by those critical of her success. Her genre-switching albums are beloved by millions and she takes great joy at reclaiming exactly who she is in songs like 'We Are Never Ever Getting Back Together' – in which she acknowledges she's made a mistake by getting together with someone who wasn't right for her. It's the same idea with dating someone who doesn't 'get you' in her song 'You Belong With Me' – if a relationship is meant to be it will be, and if not, it's probably for the best.

Think of a time when you did something you regret. When you want to leave something behind, it can be helpful to think about positive things you learned from the experience. Are there any lessons you can learn from the mistake? Use this space to reflect and write them down.

What other ways can you leave something behind? What helps you find closure? Jot down a few ideas that might help you leave behind a time you associate with regret.

Patience

Many of us are convinced that we need to have everything figured out in order to be happy. We are always looking towards the next milestone or the next goal, believing that once we achieve that one thing our lives will be perfect. But we need to be patient. 'A Place in This World' is a tune that serves as a good reminder that life is a journey, not a destination, that you don't have to have everything figured out at any given moment. It isn't always about looking towards the future but rather enjoying the road you are proudly strutting down, flicking your hair, wearing your sparkly cowboy boots and smiling with each step.

What future pressures do you put yourself under? Are you always looking forward and thinking life will be sorted once you have your next assignment done, or that a promotion at work will suddenly make everything better? Be honest and list things you are grateful for in your life right now.

Make a list of things you have achieved that you convinced yourself would make your life better. Now consider, have they? Did you celebrate reaching these milestones or did you continue to want 'more'.

_____

_____

_____

_____

_____

_____

_____

Taylor tip: Embrace your boundaries and put your own peace first. For example: practise self-compassion and try to avoid harsh self-judgement; prioritize self-care, taking time to engage in activities that bring you physical and/ or mental contentment; try to limit comparisons with others and focus on your own personal growth instead.

Lavender Haze

Do you sometimes feel there isn't enough colour in your life? Is it time for some red lippy? Or maybe you need to embrace Taylor's nail trend and paint each fingernail a colour that represents a time in your life? Sometimes we can get so lost in our daily lives we forget that our outfits and colour choices can reflect on where we are and what vibes we are putting out to the world. Taylor has long loved colours as symbolism and her songs are full of colourful mentions, where she uses them as a storytelling device or as metaphors for various feelings and emotions. What's your favourite colour? Do you own anything of that colour now — in your wardrobe, as an accessory, somewhere in your home? If not, why not?

If you could describe your mood right now as a colour, what would it be? Why? What colour would your friends and family say you are?

_____

_____

_____

_____

_____

_____

_____

_____

_____

_____

_____

_____

_____

What colours make you smile? What colours do you never wear and why? What do they remind you of?

_____

_____

_____

_____

_____

_____

_____

_____

_____

_____

Taylor tip: If you don't want a wardrobe overhaul, why not shop for some colourful accessories? Friendship bracelets are a nice touch with a hint of colour.

Karma's a Relaxing Thought

Just as Taylor has had to do many times, there is class in rising above situations, however public or damaging you feel they might be. And Taylor displays a positive side to the idea, too, not just by focusing on revenge and horrible people getting their comeuppance but by showcasing all the good things and valuable people she has in her life now as a result of her positive actions and healthy intentions. Sometimes the best course of action is to tune out the noise of the people around you who criticize and moan, and to focus on your own dreams and all the good karma you've earned by being a good person.

Read or research more about karma and what it means to different people. Do you believe in karma? What aspects of it can you relate to?

_____

_____

_____

_____

_____

_____

_____

_____

_____

_____

_____

_____

_____

_____

Next time you want to retaliate or take a swipe at someone who has upset you, take a moment to close your eyes and count to ten. By the time you get to one, are you really still angry or can you smile and walk away as a victor? Write down how you feel different after taking some time to breathe.

Taylor tip: Do you need a regular social media cull? Listen to 'You Need to Calm Down': Taylor knows all about keyboard warriors and how they aren't worth her time. Instead, think about if there are any more positive accounts you can follow, to bring some brightness and positivity into your day.

The Show Must Go On

Taylor's music isn't just to be heard remotely through a radio or headphones in a bedroom. Her sell-out tours are just that because the singer knows performing to her fans is what it's all about and she has made a commitment to them. 'I Can Do It with a Broken Heart' is about the relatable idea that sometimes in life we have to conquer our emotions, barriers, anxieties and issues we think we won't be able to overcome – and show that when we put our minds to it, we can push through. We are tougher than we think, and it's worth remembering the times you showed up, the times you dug deep and your show went on because you made a commitment or promise to do it. Take strength from those times.

Take some time to journal about how you help yourself when you come up against barriers. For example, can you assess a situation with a logical mind or do you find your emotional side takes over? How do you communicate in these situations? Do you find it helps to talk? To plan? To brainstorm? Do you find you try to shut yourself away from a situation or relationship if things become too hard?

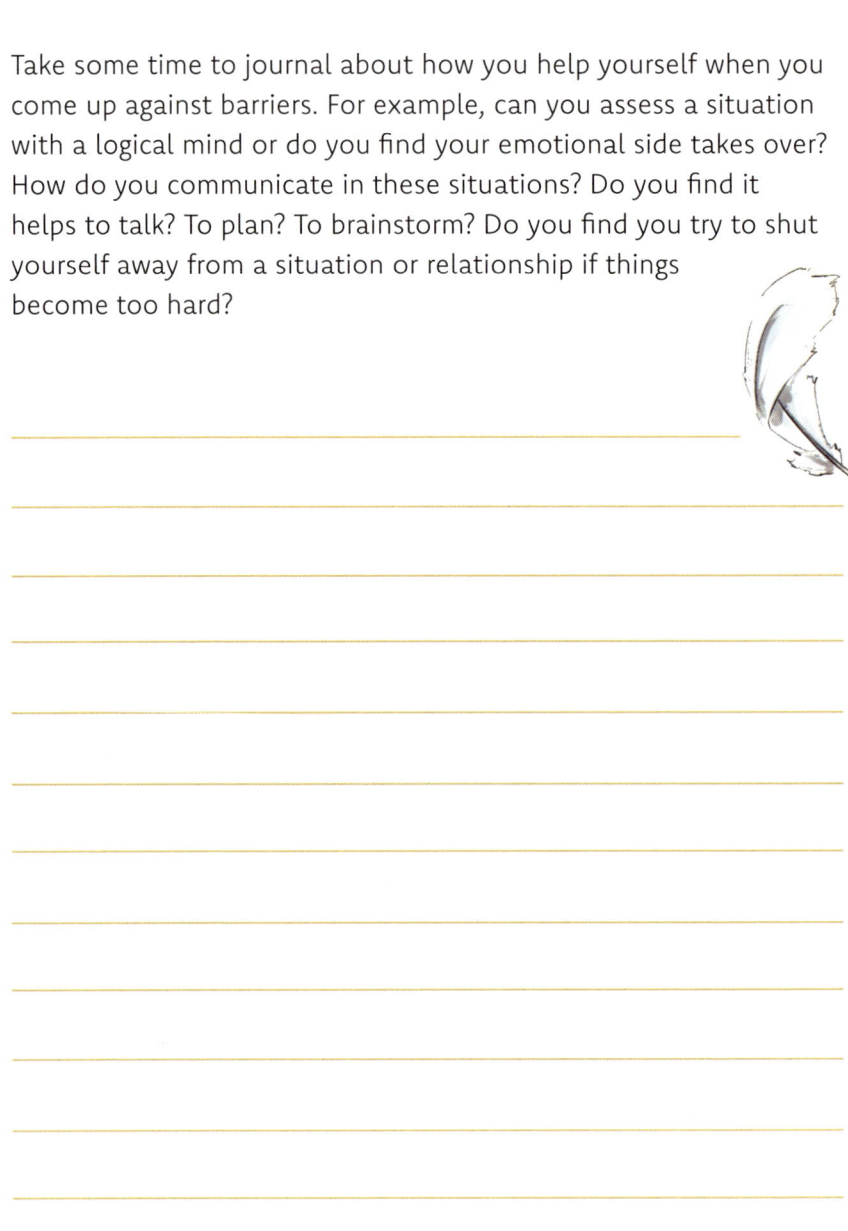

How do you tend to react when you encounter difficult situations?
If you stumble over something, do you automatically give up?
Think about those situations and record how you might act
differently if they happened to you again.

Follow Your Instincts

Ever had one of those moments when your gut told you something wasn't right? Or do you get feelings about a person and the bad energy they are surrounded by the moment you meet them? In 'We Are Never Ever Getting Back Together' Taylor lists clues that a relationship isn't going to work, like a partner being dismissive of your music taste. And 'The Moment I Knew', a song Taylor wrote about the second she knew a relationship wasn't going to work, is a nod to that wonderful intuition sense we like to ignore. But why do we ignore it when it sends us such clear and strong messages? Maybe it's time to listen to our inner voices, our sixth sense, that niggling vibe, just a little bit more ...

What times have you ignored your gut feelings about a situation or person? Can you explain moments when your inner voice has guided you? What feelings do you get when you know something isn't right?

List situations that you avoid for their bad vibes and energy, and don't be afraid to say no if these situations rear up again — you have the power to trust your gut and say no. What things make you feel good in your gut? List those too, and think about how you can engineer more of those good gut experiences in your life.

_____

_____

_____

_____

_____

_____

_____

_____

_____

_____

_____

_____

Have Wild Dreams

'Wildest Dreams' embodies the idea that relationships, no matter how much we want them to last, are sometimes just snapshots of a moment in time and not permanent — however much we hope they will be. Perhaps the underlying message here is that you should never stop aiming for your biggest dreams (whether that is embarking on a new relationship or in another area of your life, like your work), and you shouldn't avoid doing something because it might be over before you want it to be. This way of thinking can help you when it comes to setting your sights high, shooting for your dreams and always being willing to accept the next challenge that might come along.

Failure is a very normal part of trying anything new. Are you going to stop trying to achieve something (a promotion or a new career path or even a fitness goal) just because of temporary setbacks? Always keep in mind that you can do hard things — write down some times you have 'failed' on your journey towards achieving something. How did you overcome the challenges to keep chasing your dream?

Can you break down your 'dreams' into more manageable targets? What are they? How can you take steps towards them and feel that you have got to a natural end (success!) before you move on to the next target?

Taylor tip: Share your past failures with other people — widely through social media or more personally with your closest friends. What about them do you think really 'failed'? Do other people agree or challenge your idea of what's failed?

The Best Day

Taylor's tribute song to her mother is a reminder that mums make everything better. Whether that's always knowing what to say when we need some comfort, just being there and showing up when we need them, or having fun and accompanying us to gigs, where would we be without them? But how often do we express this or even acknowledge their influence? Parents are the backbone of who we are, as are grandparents or any relatives or chosen family members who have taught or influenced us, simply making our life a little brighter just by being in it.

Write your parents or other strong influences in your life a letter, thanking them for particular childhood memories you hold dear and telling them why they are special to you.

_____

_____

_____

_____

_____

_____

_____

_____

_____

_____

_____

_____

Write down three things you are grateful for about your childhood —
how have those things influenced your life and who you are right
at this moment?.

Taylor tip: Plan some 'best days'. Spend uninterrupted,
quality time with your parents or older members
of your family. Just because you can.

Make Today the Day

In 'All Too Well', Taylor sings about her regrets for an important relationship in her life being long in the past, now only a memory. She mentions her dad's worry at seeing her upset when she should be happy ... Parents have a natural instinct to want to protect us, and it's important to try to stay open and honest with them as we get older and our struggles become more complex.

The people who love us won't always be there to protect us — life has a strange way of zooming by, and before you know it, the people we think to ourselves we must call or message or catch up with are suddenly a distant memory. If you could talk to anyone right now, who would it be and why? Your friends, family and loved ones you haven't seen for a while don't deserve to be dismissed as an 'another day' activity. Make today the day.

Going back to the question of who you would like to talk to right now, make a list of friends and family members you haven't met up with for a while. Who would love a quick message or a thoughtful card posted to them? Or maybe an invite out for a pumpkin spiced latte? Make a list of people and the activities you could do together and start reaching out.

Don't wait until New Year to make a resolution list — start making one in the space below with an objective of linking you and your family members with different activities — Go-karting with Auntie Jaz? Booked!

_____

_____

_____

_____

_____

_____

_____

_____

_____

_____

Taylor tip: Why not set up a family messaging group so that you can share photos, experiences, memories or thoughts at any time?

Never Grow Up

Listening to a song about the joys and heartbreaks of being a teenager in Taylor's song 'Fifteen' is a good reminder to us all that our younger years are tough, that we don't always know what to do or how to act, or where we fit in this big wide world – but that's OK!

The tune 'Never Grow Up' reminds us that getting older can be scary and full of uncertainties – you will make mistakes, get things wrong and realize that not everyone is on your side. But that's OK. Sometimes you just have to forge ahead, and you'll find that creating your own path independently is an amazing achievement. There will be plenty of good moments ahead of you if you can keep going through the difficult times – the ride might be bumpy, but it will be worth it.

What things did you enjoy doing when you were younger and wish you still did? What opportunities can you involve yourself in to recreate them again? Think about the child-like joy those activities gave you when you were younger — what could you do now to capture those feelings again?

_____

_____

_____

_____

_____

_____

_____

_____

_____

_____

_____

_____

_____

Taylor tip: Look back on old family albums or photos with friends or family and recall adventures you had — what would you do again? What would you do differently?

Me

Our parents know and love us for being exactly who we are — a personal uniqueness that is celebrated in the self-worth promoting song 'ME!' Just like the song is an anthem of empowerment and self-love, the message here is that sometimes you can just enjoying living in the moment, that fun songs can make us feel good and put us in a better mood, and that if you like what you are doing, keep doing it!

Find ways you can practise healthy self-love, ways in which you can treat yourself with compassion and kindness, the same way you would treat your friends. Make a list of things you can do to bring you a sense of joy, calm and peace.

Think about areas of your life you'd like to embrace further. Do you need to turn your attention to your health? Could you do more exercise? What are you talented at that you would like to get even better at? What makes you, you?

Taylor tip: Embrace your gentle era and find things that you love and get enjoyment from, rather than things that annoy you. Focus on the things you love.

What Would Marjorie Do?

Taylor's grandmother, Marjorie Finlay, was an opera singer and was very close to Taylor, which is why the singer released a song in her honour in 2020. The song 'Marjorie' touches on all the advice Taylor remembers being given by her grandmother, with the lyrics a reminder that you can be both strong and kind and that knowing your worth is key to harnessing your power. Advice we are given by our parents or grandparents comes from a place of knowledge, from experiences, and having strong and inspiring women in her family is something Taylor loves to celebrate.

What advice or sayings do you use or remember from your grandparents? Jot them down here.

_____

_____

_____

_____

_____

_____

If you could pass on any advice to the next generation, what would it be?

_____

_____

_____

_____

_____

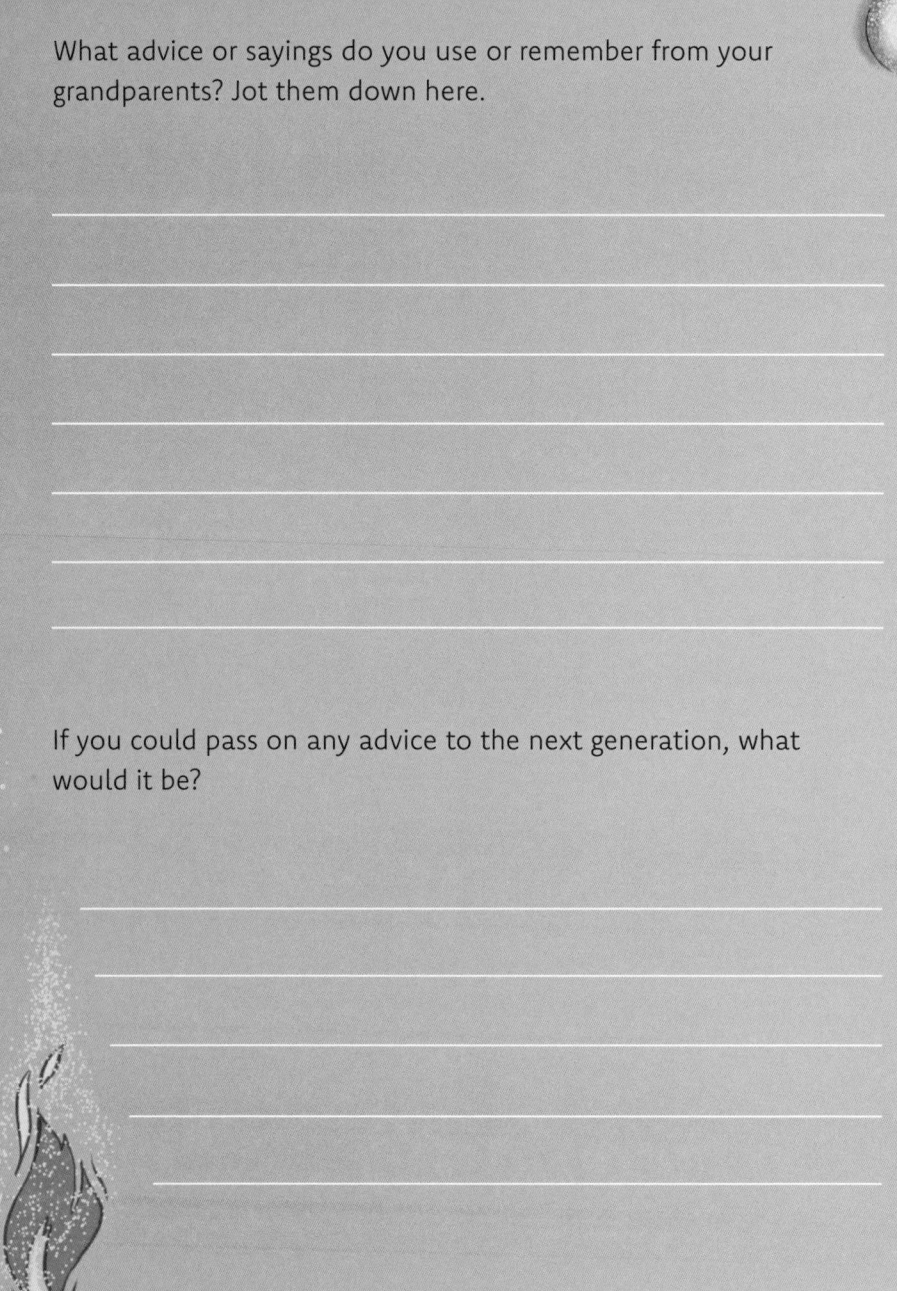

What have you found to be important as you get older? Do you miss some activities you used to do with your grandparents that are harder to recreate now? Perhaps there are certain hobbies or pursuits you could continue to do? Or were there certain things you did with a parent or grandparent that you have stopped doing but really miss?

_____

_____

_____

_____

_____

_____

_____

_____

_____

_____

The Eighties

This decade's sound was iconic — the likes of Madonna, Whitney Houston and Tina Turner, to name a few! If you lived it and loved it, you'll know exactly how good the music was. If the hits of that era aren't in your music memory, Taylor brings the sound firmly into the present and mixes the old and new together in celebration. This is probably why her music started to appeal not just to young fans but to their mums and older relatives too. This nod to bringing people together is important in life. Sometimes we get so fixated on our own lives, we forget the ones that have played a pivotal role in shaping us, so here's a chance to celebrate with loved ones using a combined love of music — and dance the night away!

What musical influences have shaped your life? What songs do you remember from your childhood? Write down your favourites, put on the tracks that have defined your years and share them with a family member.

_____

_____

_____

_____

_____

_____

_____

_____

_____

_____

_____

_____

_____

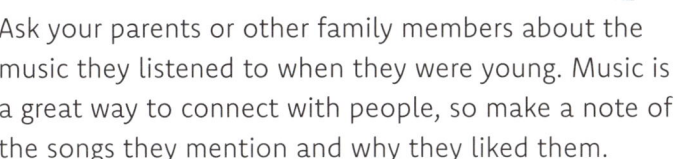

Ask your parents or other family members about the music they listened to when they were young. Music is a great way to connect with people, so make a note of the songs they mention and why they liked them.

Taylor tip: Ask your family to seek out old records and albums and invite them round to play them. Throw an eighties-themed party or celebrate music from another era that stands out.

Wear Only Yourself

Remember when you were a kid and you got to wear a princess dress or a tutu whenever you wanted? Or maybe you have a colourful sequinned playsuit that you bought ages ago but have yet to find an occasion to wear? The occasion is now! Taylor's tour costumes, award show dresses and music video outfits all embrace her different incarnations and how they portray her personality. So, if you want to go out dressed in your fanciest thigh-high boots or a floaty number — this is the time to do it. Clothes can portray a great sense of optimism, excitement and fun — so if you want to go to a fancy dress party as a portion of French fries, go for it. You don't need anyone's permission.

What are your dream outfits or styles for next season? List them here. You could even draw them or cut out pictures from magazines.

_____

_____

_____

_____

_____

_____

_____

_____

Taylor tip: Declutter your wardrobe. Do you have multiple versions of the same thing? Send duplicates to a charity shop or pass them on to friends, because the more you have of the same types of clothes, the more likely you won't wear anything else!

Are there certain eras you most relate to and do you have clothes/ outfits that represent those eras? What about celebrating those eras in your home decor too? Write down the things you most relate to from each era.

A Lesson Learned

Standing your ground isn't about being difficult. Sometimes, a journey of self-growth means demonstrating that some fights are worth having. Growing up in an unforgiving industry meant there was no shortage of difficult lessons Taylor had to learn along the way. In her feisty, modern-day women's anthem 'Bejeweled', she reminds us that affirming your self-value is something we all need to do: we are who we are, and we have no need to make any apology for that. So, be open with people, be empathetic and make your voice heard. Your inextinguishable spark does not need external validation.

Write a letter to your younger self explaining some of the biggest challenges you have had to face in your life — but also how you overcame them and the lessons you learned. How did you change for the better after those experiences?

Taylor tip: Reach out on social media with some inspiring posts that show even darker moments can be overcome – even if it's only to a small group of friends, you never know who might feel inspired reading them.

Make Art Your Plan

Follow in Taylor's footsteps and lean into the times when you've struggled, felt pain and hit rock bottom. Some of the singer's best albums have come out of the darkest of times — times of heartache or break-ups and the stages you go through after a relationship breakdown. Like she uses songwriting, especially in 'Down Bad' and 'Teardrops On My Guitar', as her way of expressing those times, there are lots of ways you can focus on finding inspiration, too. Taylor's favourite ways are reading voraciously and writing list upon list of words she loves, conversations she overhears or arguments she's had. Her method of making art is inspiration to try to use some aspect of even the trickiest times in our lives for some good.

Write down some song lyrics that you personally connect with.
How do they make you feel?

_____

_____

_____

_____

_____

_____

_____

_____

_____

_____

_____

_____

_____

_____

_____

_____

For Taylor, her emotions come out as she exercises at the gym. What hobbies help you to get in touch with your emotions? Try journalling afterwards — how do your hobbies help you process your emotions?

_____

_____

_____

_____

_____

_____

_____

_____

_____

Taylor tip: Cut up old bits of fabric that feel nice to touch and gather together colours and patterns that you are drawn to from notecards and magazines. Collect all these bits of material as the starting point to a mood board.

Create your mood board full of beautiful photos/designs/
people/places that you are drawn to. There doesn't need
to be any sort of rhyme or reason as to why you chose
the different elements, only that they speak to your soul
and you feel motivated, inspired or calmed by them.

Embrace Your Anti-hero

Learning how to embrace the bits of yourself you don't like and thinking about how you can reframe them isn't a quick or easy fix, but it might help you recognize that even traits that are seen as ugly aren't always bad. Ugly feelings, like getting jealous over a friend's supposedly ideal lifestyle or getting angry about a situation, don't make you an ugly person. Take some time to think about how you react to things and why, and instead of thinking they are 'negatives', list them as your unique traits. For example: are you stubborn? Great, you know your own mind! Do you feel overwhelmed at social gatherings? Good for you, you are confident in knowing you like your own company.

Make a list of things you think are your worst personality traits. Now decorate those words. Add colour or patterns and shapes.

Draw lines out from these words and think about times when these traits have been a positive — maybe even heroic — and aren't actually negative.

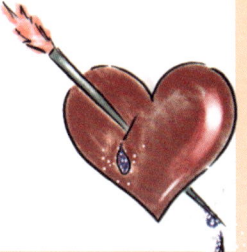

Sorry, What?

Taylor once admitted that she is trying through her music to help men learn how to apologize for their problematic actions and behaviours, and this stems from the idea that women are programmed to say sorry a lot more than necessary. Her feminist track 'The Man' sees Taylor imagine how she would be treated if she wasn't a woman, reminding us there are no characteristics that should be held in different esteem for men or women. As women, we are bosses, we are truthful, we stand up for what we believe in and we call out untruths, because that's what makes good people, regardless of gender. Taylor doesn't need to apologize for singing songs others don't like. And for the haters, it's those songs that have made her a billionaire!

Write a list of times when you have felt the need to say sorry over something that wasn't your fault. Can you identify common themes: do you always apologize if you get interrupted in a work meeting? What if you've said something you know to be true but which others have been taken aback by? Perhaps you hide your competitive streak too much and it's time to unleash it more? If you find yourself wanting to be more direct but fear this is a bad thing, it's not!

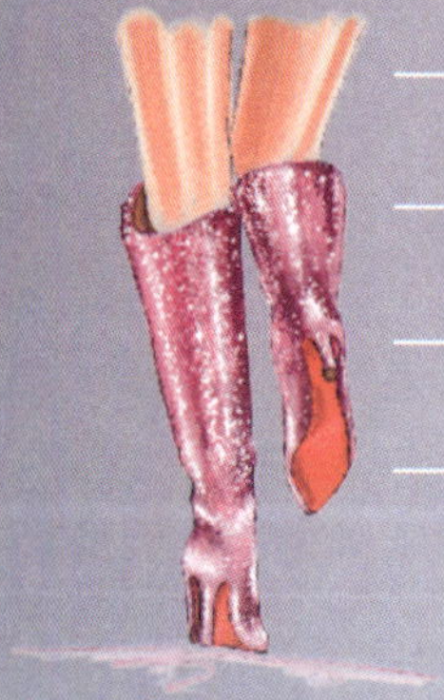

_____

_____

_____

_____

_____

_____

_____

_____

_____

_____

Taylor tip: Practise staying silent when you would normally apologize. It might take time to get used to, so start counting to ten in your head to make a conscious effort not to blurt out, 'I'm sorry!'

State of Grace

The idea of confronting something you never thought you would be able to do but going ahead and doing it anyway is a theme in Taylor's compelling tune 'State of Grace'. Seizing the day is an idea that might scare and thrill you in equal measure, but what's the worst that can happen?

In both her 2020 lockdown albums, Taylor invents fictional characters to create worlds and opportunities that aren't biographical but rather magical fantasies and unexplored ideas. You don't need to transform your life in such a grand way to experience new things; sometimes small tweaks can open up a world of opportunity.

Research activities you've always wanted to try and where you can do them. Create your own world of fictional characters or versions of you and see where it leads you — can you see yourself as one of the characters embarking on a new adventure? Draw up a list of adventure ideas and write about the kind of person who might do those things.

_____

_____

_____

_____

_____

_____

_____

_____

_____

_____

_____

_____

_____

Record what new activities you enjoyed — is there anything you still want to achieve?

_____

_____

_____

_____

_____

_____

_____

_____

Taylor tip: Find volunteering opportunities that broaden your mind. Taylor puts a lot of importance on giving back to society, donating money to foodbanks and to schools to improve education. Could you be inspired? Maybe volunteer at your local library or hold a second-hand book sale and donate the money to your local school?

About the Author

Abi Smith is a former showbiz and celebrity journalist and travel writer, and has written fifteen published books for adults and children in the world of sport, celebrity and lifestyle.

About the Illustrator

Alicia Nicole is a fashion illustrator based in Oxfordshire. Her work is sold internationally and she has collaborated with brands to create fashion illustrations for social media-focused campaigns and live-sketch events. Fashion art school ignited Alicia's love for fashion illustration/artwork. She always loved drawing but found her niche at university, exploring different fashion illustration techniques and artists. Alicia draws inspiration primarily from strong, powerful women adorned in stunning outfits. Most of her work is meticulously hand-rendered using artist-quality illustration markers, but she also enjoys creating digital drawings.